GW00889107

Level 3

Workbook

Alistair McCallum

OXFORD
UNIVERSITY PRESS

Remember this?

1 Fill in the blanks with *in*, *on* or *at*.

ARGENTINA VS. MEXICO

Sunday June 26th 2005, 6:00 p.m.

1 The match was __in__ 2005.

2 It was _____ June.

3 It started _____ 6:00 p.m.

4 It wasn't _____ the morning. It was _____ the evening.

5 It was _____ June 26th.

6 It was _____ Sunday.

2 Fill in the blanks with *too* or *not enough* and the adjectives in parentheses.

1 That car won't win the race. It is _n't fast enough_____. (fast)

2 That laptop costs $2,000. I can't buy it. It's _____. (expensive)

3 She's only 14. She can't drive. She is _____. (old)

4 I don't want to go in the swimming pool. It's _____. (cold)

5 We can't have a party for 200 people! Our house is _____. (big)

3 Fill in the blanks with the *-ing* form of the verb.

1 Alberto enjoys _____dancing_____. (dance)

2 I love _____. (windsurf)

3 _____ in a big city is exciting. (live)

4 I don't like _____. It's boring! (shop)

5 Carol is good at _____ the guitar. (play)

6 I hate _____ up early! (get)

4 Circle the correct words.

1 I **wasn't** / **weren't** at school last week. I had a sore throat.

2 Where **was** / **were** you last weekend?

3 My parents **wasn't** / **weren't** at home yesterday evening.

4 Jessica **was** / **were** in New York last summer.

5 Why **was** / **were** the teacher angry with you this morning?

6 I **was** / **were** at Mark's house last Saturday.

5 Look at Rita's diary for last Saturday. Fill in the blanks in the conversation. Use the simple past.

SATURDAY

10:00 tennis

12:00 Lunch (Pizza House)

7:00 Tanya

8:00 concert

You: (1)_____Did you play_____ soccer in the morning? (you / play)

Rita: No, I didn't. I (2)_____ tennis.

You: Where (3)_____ lunch? (you / have)

Rita: I (4)_____ lunch at Pizza House.

You: (5)_____ Robbie in the evening? (you / meet)

Rita: No, I (6)_____. I (7)_____ Tanya.

You: Where (8)_____? (you / go)

Rita: We (9)_____ to a concert.

You: What time (10)_____ _____? (the concert / start)

Rita: It (11)_____ at eight o'clock.

6 Fill in the blanks with the correct words below.

> can   can't   don't have to   have to   should   shouldn't

1 Do you have a toothache? You _____*should*_____ visit the dentist.
2 It's a holiday today. We _____ go to school. We _____ go to the beach!
3 You _____ go to bed late. You have school in the morning.
4 When you travel to another country, you _____ take your passport.
5 Joe doesn't have a ticket. He _____ go to the soccer match.

7 Fill in the blanks. Make adverbs from the adjectives in parentheses.

1 The children are playing ____*happily*____. (happy)

2 He plays the violin _____. (good)

3 She shouted _____. (angry)

4 They talked _____. (quiet)

5 He sometimes drives _____. (fast)

6 I think he'll pass the exam _____. (easy)

8 Complete the puzzle.

1 I love writing. I want a _____*career*_____ as a journalist.
2 When I'm in London, I'm going to buy some _____.
3 Before you start your job, you have to _____ a contract.
4 Christina Aguilera recorded her first _____ in 1999.
5 I was born in France, but I speak Spanish because I _____ up in Spain.
6 This street is a mess. Everyone drops _____!

What's the mystery word? _____

Unit 1

Vocabulary

1 Match the sentences with the adjectives.

1 "I know I'm going to pass the exam. I've worked hard!"   a shy

2 "I like telling jokes and stories, and I love parties!"   b helpful

3 "I'm the best student in this college!"   c fun

4 "I don't like parties. I'm nervous when I meet new people."   d pushy

5 "I run five kilometers every day."   e confident

6 "Be quiet, everybody! Let me speak!"   f daring

7 "That bag looks heavy. Can I carry it for you?"   g arrogant

8 "I love parachuting and shark diving!"   h fit

2 Fill in the blanks with the adjectives below.

> cheerful   friendly   hard-working   lazy   punctual   sympathetic

What are they like?

1 Marco always arrives on time.
He's _____*punctual*_____.

2 Visitors are always welcome at Tina's house.
She's _____.

3 Danilo's a builder. He never stops!
He's _____.

4 Marina always listens to people's problems.
She's _____.

5 Jessica always looks happy.
She's _____.

6 Dan never helps with the housework.
He's _____.

Extend your vocabulary

4

Grammar

1 Match the questions with the answers.

1 What does he look like? _d_
2 What's she like? ___
3 What are they like? ___
4 What does she look like? ___
5 What's he like? ___
6 What do they look like? ___

a They're friendly.
b He's fit and daring.
c She's short and she has curly hair.
d He's tall and slim.
e They're tall and they have dark hair.
f She's hard-working.

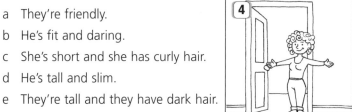

2 Fill in the blanks in these questions. Use *is, are, do* or *does*.

1 A: What ___'s___ your best friend like?
   B: She's very sympathetic and fun.
2 A: What _____ your teacher look like?
   B: He's tall and overweight.
3 A: What _____ your neighbors like?
   B: They're very friendly.
4 A: What _____ your brother like?
   B: He's lazy.
5 A: What _____ your parents look like?
   B: They're short and they have dark hair.

3 Look at the chart. Complete the questions and answers.

Name:	Maria	Hans	Micky and Dicky
Appearance:	tall, curly hair	overweight, strong	short, dark hair
Personality:	confident, hard-working	sensible, helpful	fun, friendly

1 A: What's Maria like?
   B: She's ___confident___ and hard-working.
2 A: What _____ Hans look like?
   B: He's _____ and _____ .
3 A: What _____ Micky and Dicky like?
   B: They're _____ and friendly.
4 A: _____ Maria look like?
   B: _____ and she has curly hair.
5 A: _____ Hans like?
   B: _____ .
6 A: _____ Micky and Dicky look _____ ?
   B: _____ .

Vocabulary

1 Label the pictures with the words below.

What are they made of?

| cotton   leather   metal   plastic   wood   wool |

1 a handbag: _____leather_____

2 a T-shirt: _____

3 a CD: _____

4 a key: _____

5 a box: _____

6 a scarf: _____

What are they like?

| patterned   plain   striped |

7 _____

8 _____

9 _____

---

2 Fill in the blanks with the adjectives below.

| comfortable   flexible   light   transparent   waterproof |

1 I love my sneakers. They're really _____comfortable_____!

2 My watch is _____. I can swim with it!

3 This radio is really cool – it's _____!

4 I can carry this surfboard easily. It's _____.

5 These glasses are amazing. They're _____.

Extend your vocabulary

Grammar

1 **Put the words in order to make questions.**

1 is / your surfboard / long / how ?

  _How long is your surfboard_____ ?

  It's 2.5 meters.

2 like / your cell phone / what's ?

  _____ ?

  It's small and light.

3 of / what's / made / this bag ?

  _____ ?

  It's made of plastic.

4 that laptop / heavy / how / is ?

  _____ ?

  It's 2 kilograms.

5 made / your skirt / of / what's ?

  _____ ?

  It's made of wool.

6 what's / like / your skateboard ?

  _____ ?

  It's old and heavy.

2 **Fill in the blanks in the questions with the words below.**

> big   ~~how~~   like   made   of   what's

1 __How__ tall is your teacher?

2 _____ your guitar like?

3 What's your T-shirt _____ of?

4 What's your camera _____ ?

5 How _____ is your bike?

6 What's that surfboard made _____ ?

3 **Look at these pictures, then complete the conversations.**

1 Ken: _What's_ that skateboard _made of_ ?

  Meg: It's made of wood and metal.

2 Ken: _____ long is it?

  Meg: It's 80 centimeters.

3 Ken: _____ heavy _____ ?

  Meg: It weighs 2 kilograms.

4 Renata: _____ your new coat like?

  Atsuko: It's really cool!

5 Renata: _____ it _____ ?

  Atsuko: It's made of leather.

6 Richard: _____ your new car _____ ?

  Jeremy: It's great!

7 Richard: _____ fast _____ ?

  Jeremy: It goes 150 kilometers per hour.

8 Richard: _____ big _____ ?

  Jeremy: It's enormous!

Unit 2

Vocabulary

1 Write the missing verbs in the phrases below.
Then write them in the crossword.

1 → ___chew___ gum
1 ↓ _____ on a test
2 _____ a fan letter
3 → _____ an appointment
3 ↓ _____ in love
4 _____ someone's e-mail
5 _____ a practical joke
6 _____ a lie

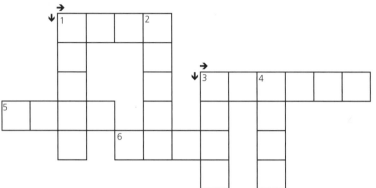

2 Match the phrases below with the pictures.

> break a window   eat too much cake   have a bad toothache
> fall off a bike   meet a movie star   see a crocodile

1 ___meet a movie star___

2 _____

3 _____

4 _____

5 _____

6 _____

Extend your vocabulary

Grammar

1 Write the past participles of these regular and irregular verbs.

Regular		Irregular	
work ➜ *worked*		fall ➜ *fallen*	
play ➜ _____		do ➜ _____	
cheat ➜ _____		forget ➜ _____	
watch ➜ _____		have ➜ _____	
cook ➜ _____		see ➜ _____	

2 Fill in the blanks with *have* or *has*.

1 ___*Have*___ you ever forgotten your homework?

2 _____ John ever had an accident?

3 I _____ never fallen off my bike.

4 My parents _____ never been to the U.S.

5 Marie _____ never met a movie star.

3 Look at the chart. Write sentences with *never* about the people in the chart.

	Juan	Sandra	Mark	Karen
tell a lie	yes	yes	never	never
read a friend's e-mail	never	yes	never	yes
cheat on an exam	yes	never	yes	never
write a fan letter	yes	never	never	yes
have an accident	never	yes	yes	never

1 Juan / read a friend's e-mail

   Juan has never read a friend's e-mail _____.

2 Sandra / cheat on an exam

   _____.

3 Karen / have an accident

   _____.

4 Sandra and Mark / write a fan letter

   _____

   _____.

5 Mark and Karen / tell a lie

   _____

   _____.

4 Write questions with *ever* about the people in the chart. Write the answers, too.

1 Juan and Sandra / tell a lie

   Have Juan and Sandra ever ___*told a lie*___?

   Yes, they have.

2 Juan / cheated on an exam

   Has Juan ever _____?

   Yes, _____.

3 Sandra / write a fan letter

   _____?

   _____, _____.

4 Sandra and Karen / read a friend's e-mail

   _____?

   _____, _____.

5 Juan and Karen / have an accident

   _____?

   _____, _____.

Vocabulary

1 **Read the definitions. Then unscramble the words in the expressions.**

1	do something wrong	➜	make a imsatek	_mistake_
2	decide	➜	make a iconides	_____
3	do something different	➜	make a ghecan	_____
4	prepare for something	➜	make a nalp	_____
5	tell people about your idea	➜	make a nesutgiogs	_____
6	give money or gifts	➜	make a idannoto	_____
7	tell everybody what you're going to do	➜	make an comentanenun	_____

2 **What are the people saying? Match the expressions below with the pictures.**

Come in!   Get down!   Get out!   Get up!   Look out!   Sit up!

1 _____ _Sit up!_ _____

2 _____

3 _____

4 _____

5 _____

6 _____

Extend your vocabulary

Grammar

1 **Circle the correct words.**

1 I'm not going to learn the piano this year.
I've **already** / **yet** decided to learn the guitar.

2 I haven't received my exam results **already** / **yet**.

3 I'm not hungry. I've **just** / **yet** had lunch.

4 I can't go out. I haven't finished my homework **already** / **yet**.

5 I've **already** / **yet** seen *Party Animal*. Let's watch another movie.

2 **Write sentences with *just*.**

1 Donna / buy / a new laptop
Donna has just bought a new laptop .

2 Colin / win / the tennis match
_____ .

3 they / walk / ten kilometers
_____ .

4 Hernando / see / a scary movie
_____ .

3 **Look at the pictures, then complete the sentences with *already* and *yet*.**

(put away – clothes)

1 Atsuko hasn't ___*put away her clothes yet*___ .

2 Ricky has *already* _____ .

(pack – bags)

3 Gavin hasn't _____ his bags _____ .

4 Anita has _____ .

(finish – the test)

5 Luisa and Tony _____ .

6 Enzo and Mary _____ .

Unit 3

Vocabulary

1 Circle (→ or ↓) the six verbs in the wordsearch. Then fill in the blanks in the sentences below.

I'm going to visit my friends in London next month. I've never been to England before!

1 I'm going to ___*apply*___ for a passport tomorrow.

2 My parents are going to _____ a flight for me.

3 I'm going to _____ my bags soon.

4 When I leave, my classmates are going to _____ me off at the airport.

5 When I arrive in London, I'm not going to _____ a taxi.

6 My friends are going to _____ me up at the airport.

E	T	U	A	D	F
O	A	P	P	L	Y
Y	K	L	I	A	B
S	E	V	C	M	O
P	A	C	K	L	O
D	R	S	E	E	K

2 Match the pictures with the phrases below.

> apartment   hotel   motel   tent   camper   youth hostel

1 ___*motel*___

2 _____

3 _____

4 _____

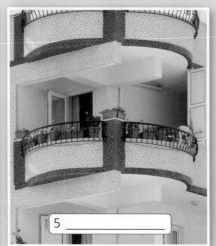

5 _____

6 _____

Extend your vocabulary

Grammar

1 Are these people talking about plans or are they making offers? Check (✔) one box for each sentence.

	Plan	Offer
1 "I'm going to visit England next month."	✔	☐
2 "We'll pick you up at the airport."	☐	✔
3 "Is that case heavy? I'll carry it for you."	☐	☐
4 "I'm going to buy a new cellphone this afternoon."	☐	☐
5 "Fiona's going to have a party next week."	☐	☐
6 "Come to the movie with me! I'll buy a ticket for you."	☐	☐
7 "Tim and Serena are going to start a rock band."	☐	☐
8 "Are you hungry? I'll cook a pizza!"	☐	☐

2 Look at these students' plans for next Saturday. Then fill in the blanks with *(not) going to* and the verbs in parentheses.

1 Barbara _is going to do_ (do) her homework on Saturday morning.

2 Ken _isn't going to have_ (not have) a guitar lesson on Saturday morning. He _____ (have) a piano lesson.

3 Barbara and Debbie _____ (have) lunch at twelve o'clock.

4 Ken _____ (go) to Maria's party in the evening.

5 Barbara _____ (not play) computer games in the evening. She _____ (see) a movie.

6 Ken and Omar _____ (not play) soccer at two o'clock. They _____ (play) tennis.

Ken
Next Saturday:
morning - piano lesson
2:00 - tennis with Omar
evening - Maria's party
Barbara
Next Saturday:
morning - homework!!!
12:00 - lunch with Debbie
(Dino's café)
evening - movie

3 Fill in the blanks in these sentences. Use *going to* and *will*.

1 A: _I'm going to have_ a party next week, but I don't know what CDs to play.

   B: _I'll_ help you choose. I love music!

2 A: _____ visit Cathy's house tomorrow, but I don't know where it is.

   B: _____ show you the way. I've been there lots of times!

3 A: _____ take the bus into town this afternoon.

   B: Don't take the bus. _____ give you a ride in my car!

Vocabulary

1 Look at the pictures. Then complete the sentences with the phrases below.

be rude   fit in   get along with   get lost   homesick for   make friends with   understand

1 I don't _understand_ Japanese!

2 I'm _____ my family!

3 Don't _____!

4 I don't like it here. I don't _____.

5 Stop laughing at that man. Don't _____.

6 It's good to _____ people when you're on vacation.

7 I _____ my host family.

Extend your vocabulary

2 Label the pictures with the words below.

confused   excited   pleased   relaxed
surprised   worried

1 _excited_   2 _____   3 _____

4 _____   5 _____   6 _____

Grammar

1 **Put the words in order to make sentences.**

1 Vicky's a strong runner. (win / she / the race / might)

   She might win the race .

2 The taxi hasn't arrived yet. (our flight / might / we / miss)

   _____ .

3 Pedro doesn't feel very well. (might / to the party / he / not / go)

   _____ .

4 My skateboard is old and heavy. (a new one / might / buy / I)

   _____ .

5 It's late and I want to go to bed. (not / my homework / finish / I / might)

   _____ .

2 **Fill in the blanks with *might* or *might not* and the verbs in parentheses.**

1 Carla is very shy. She _might not come_ (come) to the party.

2 I'm going to meet Jamie this evening. We _____ (see) a movie.

3 Those students are writing very slowly. They _____ (finish) the test.

4 I want to learn a new language this year. I _____ (study) Chinese.

5 Bob doesn't have much money. He _____ (buy) a new cellphone.

6 It's cloudy and cold. It _____ (rain) this afternoon.

3 **Write sentences with *might* or *might not* and the verbs below.**

be   get   have   like   like   speak

Alex is going to an international adventure camp. Why is he worried? What is he thinking?

1 I / the food

   I _might not like_ _the food_ .

2 The teachers / English

   _____
   _____ .

3 The other students / me

   _____
   _____ .

4 I / an accident

   _____
   _____ .

5 I / lost

   _____
   _____ .

6 The weather / terrible

   _____
   _____ .

Unit 4

Vocabulary

1 Unscramble the words in the sentences and complete the crossword.

1 I usually (ekaw) up at seven o'clock.
2 I sometimes (yerdamad) in the classroom.
3 I sometimes (medar) about flying.
4 I sometimes fall (epasle) when I'm watching TV.
5 You (wayn) when you feel sleepy.
6 I sometimes have (eramthings). They're scary.

2 Label the picture with the words below.

alarm clock   blanket   lamp   mattress   pajamas   pillow   sheet   slippers

1 _alarm clock_
2 _____
3 _____
4 _____
5 _____
6 _____
7 _____
8 _____

Extend your vocabulary

Grammar

1 Circle the correct words.

1 I **was** / **were** daydreaming in the classroom this morning.
2 You **wasn't** / **weren't** enjoying the party. Why not?
3 **Was** / **Were** your parents watching TV yesterday evening?
4 **Was** / **Were** Maria wearing her sneakers this morning?
5 The radio was on, but we **wasn't** / **weren't** listening to it.
6 José **wasn't** / **weren't** driving very fast.

2 Look at the pictures. Then fill in the blanks with the simple past form of the verbs in parentheses.

1 The taxi __*arrived*__ (arrive) at the hotel, and I _____ (pay) the taxi driver.

2 The receptionist _____ (give) me the key.

3 I _____ (walk) up the stairs and I _____ (go) into the room.

4 I _____ (open) the window and I _____ (look) out onto the street.

3 Look at the picture. Then fill in the blanks with the past progressive form of the verbs in parentheses.

It (1)_____ (not / rain). The sun (2)_____ (shine). A man (3)_____ (run) for a bus. He (4)_____ (carry) a suitcase. A girl (5)_____ (play) the guitar, and a boy (6)_____ (sing). They had a dog with them. It (7)_____ (sleep). Some students (8)_____ (sit) next to a tree. They (9)_____ (not / work). They (10)_____ _____ (have) lunch.

Vocabulary

1 Circle (→ or ↓) the eight verbs in the wordsearch. Then write the words.

P	R	E	S	S	Q	I	F
L	I	W	U	T	A	Y	R
O	T	S	T	I	C	K	E
S	E	P	A	R	A	T	E
G	A	D	D	O	L	E	Z
H	R	R	E	M	O	V	E

1 a _dd_

2 f _ _ _ _ _

3 s _ _ _ _

4 s _ _ _

5 s _ _ _ _ _ _ _

6 t _ _ _

7 p _ _ _ _

8 r _ _ _ _ _

2 What's the chef saying? Look at the pictures. Then fill in the blanks with the verbs below.

> break   burn   cook   cut   drop   pour

Cook these burgers!

2 _____ some coffee into these cups!

3 Don't _____ it!

4 Don't _____ them!

5 _____ the bread!

6 Don't _____ that glass!

Extend your vocabulary

Grammar

1 Match 1–6 with a–f.

1 I was playing soccer when
2 Jenny was talking to her classmates when
3 Paulo was walking through the sports store when
4 I was sleeping when
5 My friends were walking along the beach when

a he saw a fantastic skateboard.
b they found some money.
c the headmaster came in.
d I hurt my foot.
e the alarm clock went off.

2 Fill in the blanks with the simple past form of the verbs in parentheses.

1 She was riding her motorbike when a policeman _stopped_ her. (stop)
2 Roberto was working in the kitchen when he _____ a glass. (break)
3 The family was watching TV when dad _____ asleep. (fall)
4 You were daydreaming when the teacher _____ you a question. (ask)
5 I was lying in bed when the phone _____ . (ring)

3 Look at the pictures. Then fill in the blanks with the simple past or past progressive of the verbs in parentheses.

1 My mom _was lying_ (lie) by the hotel pool
   when it started _started_ (start) to rain.

2 I _____ (write) an e-mail when there
   _____ (be) a power cut.

3 We _____ (drive) through the woods
   when we _____ (see) a bear.

4 My dad _____ (run) along the beach
   when he _____ (fall) over.

5 My parents _____ (cook) the meal
   when their visitors _____ (arrive).

6 The waiter was _____ (carry) a tray of
   glasses when he _____ (drop) them.

Unit 5

Vocabulary

1 Find six adjectives in the word snake. Then write the adjectives below.

1 _____fast_____
2 _____
3 _____
4 _____
5 _____
6 _____

vcompetitiveoroughllenergeticefastybhardadangerousll

Write the sport hidden in the word snake: _____

Extend your vocabulary

2 Match the pictures with the phrases below.

do boxing   do fencing   do gymnastics   do the pole vault   run hurdles   throw the javelin

1 _____do boxing_____

2 _____

3 _____

4 _____

5 _____

6 _____

Grammar

1 Write the comparative form of the adjectives.

1 cold ➔ _____colder_____
2 difficult ➔ _more difficult_
3 funny ➔ _____
4 hot ➔ _____

5 tall ➔ _____
6 good ➔ _____
7 energetic ➔ _____
8 strong ➔ _____

The scooter

2 Look at the chart. Circle T (True) or F (False).

name	the scooter	the motorcycle	the sportbike
weight	115 kg	225 kg	170 kg
price	$3,199	$8,699	$10,565
length	178 cm	121 cm	202 cm
speed	85 km/h	120 km/h	250 km/h

1 The scooter is more expensive than the motorcycle. T / **F**
2 The sportbike is heavier than the scooter. T / F
3 The motorcycle is cheaper than the scooter. T / F
4 The sportbike is slower than the motorcycle. T / F
5 The scooter is longer than the motorcycle. T / F

The motorcycle

3 Fill in the blanks with the comparative form of the adjectives in parentheses.

1 The motorcycle _____is faster than_____ the scooter. (fast)
2 The scooter _____ the motorcycle. (light)
3 The sportbike _____ the motorcycle. (expensive)
4 The motorcycle _____ the scooter. (heavy)
5 The motorcycle _____ the sportbike. (short)

4 These sentences are not true. Write true sentences using *not as ... as.*

1 Soda is cheaper than water.
   No! _____Soda isn't as cheap as water_____.
2 Iceland is hotter than Argentina.
   No! _____ n't as hot _____.
3 Book 3 is easier than Book 1.
   No! _____.
4 Plastic is more expensive than gold.
   No! _____.
5 Fencing is rougher than boxing.
   No! _____.

The sportbike

Vocabulary

1 Match the words with the descriptions.

1 album
2 orchestra
3 instruments
4 tracks
5 band
6 festival

a There are a lot of these on a CD.
b A small group of musicians who play rock, pop, hip hop, etc.
c A collection of songs.
d A large group of musicians who play classical music.
e An event (usually outdoors) where a lot of musicians play.
f A guitar, a trumpet, a violin are examples of these.

2 Label the photos with the words below.

acoustic guitar   drums   electric guitar   harp   piano   saxophone   trumpet   violin

1 _violin_
2 _____
3 _____
4 _____
5 _____
6 _____
7 _____
8 _____

Extend your vocabulary

Grammar

1 Circle the correct superlative form of the adjectives.

1 *Falling Down* is the (longest)/ **most long** track on the CD.

2 Vincent weighs 65 kg. He's the **heavyest** / **heaviest** player on the team.

3 This MP3 player only costs $18. It's **cheapest** / **the cheapest** one in the store.

4 Jessie sings terribly. She's the **baddest** / **worst** singer I know!

5 Our cat weighs 15 kg. She's the **fatest** / **fattest** cat in the neighborhood!

6 In my opinion, *The World Today* is the **interestingest** / **most interesting** program on TV.

2 Fill in the blanks with the superlative form of the adjectives in bold.

1 Martha is only 17. She's a **young** person. She's _the youngest_ person in the band.

2 Those shoes cost $200. They're **expensive** shoes. They're _____ shoes in the store.

3 Mario never practices. He's a **bad** player. He's the _____ player on the team.

4 *Save the World!* is an **exciting** movie. It's _____ _____ of the year.

5 *Meet My Family* is a **funny** program. It's _____ on TV.

6 Wendy swims three kilometers every day. She's a **fit** girl. She's _____ in the school.

7 Grandpa is 85. He's an **old** person. He's _____ in our family.

3 Fill in the blanks with the superlative form of the adjectives below.

> big   difficult   fast   good   hot   lazy

1 This is _the biggest_ soccer stadium in the country.

2 Carlos is _____ _____ player on the team.

3 This is _____ _____ test of the year!

4 Justin is _____ _____ student in our class!

5 In my country, August is _____ month of the year.

6 Gina has _____ _____ car in the neighborhood!

Unit 6

Vocabulary

1 Unscramble the verbs and write them in the puzzle.

1 eb cefsusulcs
2 serercha
3 lles
4 veradiset
5 ingsed

1	b	e	s	u	c	c	e	s	s	f	u	l
2												
				3								
					a							
4												
			5									

What's the mystery word? _____

2 These people are talking about money. Fill in the blanks with the verbs below.

> borrow   donate   earn   lend   save   spend

1 I love to ___*spend*___ money!

I can't buy a ticket. I don't have any money!

2 That's OK. I'll _____ you some money.

3 I try to _____ some money to charity when I can.

HELP THE HOMELESS

4 I usually _____ some money every week. I want to buy a new skateboard!

5 I _____ a little money on the weekend. I work in the garden for two hours.

6 Dad, can I _____ some money, please?

Extend your vocabulary

Grammar

1 Circle the correct words.

1 I've lived in Manchester **(for)**/ **since** five years.
2 My cousin has played the guitar **for** / **since** 2001.
3 I love my dog. I've had him **for** / **since** three years.
4 I've lived in this city **for** / **since** last summer.
5 Jake and Roger have studied Spanish **for** / **since** two years.

2 Write questions using the words in parentheses. Then match them to the answers.

1 How long ___*have you lived*___ in La Paz? (you / live)
2 How long _____ at the garage? (Luis / work)
3 How long _____ French? (your friends / study)
4 How long _____ her cat? (your sister / have)
5 How long _____ a student? (you / be)

a She's had her cat for three years.
b I've been a student for seven years.
c I've lived in La Paz since 2001.
d They've studied French for six months.
e He's worked there for two years.

3 You're talking to Andy. Complete the conversation.

You: How long (1) *have you lived* (you / live) in New York?
Andy: (2)___*I've lived*___ in New York since 2003.

You: How long (3) _____ (you / study) Chinese?
Andy: (4) _____ Chinese for three years.

You: How long (5) _____ (you / have) a cat?
Andy: I've (6) _____ _____ six years.

You: (7) _____ (your aunt / be) a teacher?
Andy: (8) _____ _____ 1990.

You: (9)_____ (your parents / work) at the hospital?
Andy: (10) _____ _____ ten years.

You: (11) _____ (you / play) the saxophone?
Andy: (12) _____ _____ last summer.

Vocabulary

1 Circle (→ or ↓) the words and phrases in the word search. Then complete the sentences below.

S	P	E	E	C	H	M	N
Q	P	U	E	A	H	F	G
S	O	P	R	M	X	F	I
E	B	A	P	P	E	A	R
T	Y	O	H	A	A	M	A
U	E	T	I	I	R	O	I
P	D	U	R	G	S	I	S
O	R	G	A	N	I	Z	E

1 Angel Jones, the famous actress, is going to ____appear____ in a new TV show.
2 When you _____ an event, you arrange the bands, equipment, tickets and a lot of other things.
3 We're going to _____ a new organization for students. Do you want to join?
4 A charity concert can _____ a lot of money.
5 The president is going to give a _____ about human rights.
6 We're going to _____ for more money for children's homes.

2 Match the adjectives to the descriptions. Then write the correct number next to the photos.

Charities help a lot of people. For example, they help …

1 blind people   a people who don't have enough food
2 deaf people   b people who don't have a place to live
3 refugees   c people who can't see
4 homeless people   d people who can't hear
5 hungry people   e people who are trying to escape from a war
6 disabled people   f people who can't use their arms or legs

C ☐

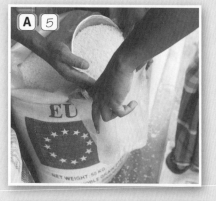

A [5]

B ☐

F ☐

D ☐

E ☐

Extend your vocabulary

Grammar

1 Circle the correct words.

1 I **bought** / **'ve bought** this cellphone in 2005.

2 *Pirates of the Caribbean* is a great movie. I **saw** / **'ve seen** it three times!

3 James loves traveling. He **visited** / **'s visited** many countries.

4 Abdul **was** / **'s been** ill yesterday.

5 I'm going to watch TV now. I **finished** / **'ve finished** my homework.

6 We **played** / **'ve played** in a band at the school concert last week.

2 Fill in the blanks with the simple past or present perfect form of the verbs in parentheses.

1 I _'ve visited_ (visit) England once. I ____went____ (go) there in 2004.

2 We _____ (play) computer games at Jon's house last Saturday.

3 My uncle is an author. He _____ (write) a lot of books.

4 Our school's soccer team _____ (win) the High School Cup twice. We _____ (won) it in 2003, and again in 2006.

5 My friend Manuel _____ (come) to see me yesterday evening.

6 My parents _____ (buy) a new car. It's cool!

3 Look at the pictures. Then complete the questions and answers. Use the words in parentheses.

A: Has David performed at the school concert?

B: Yes, he has. He (1) _'s performed_ (he / perform) at the school concert twice.

A: (2) _____ (he / play) the guitar in 2004?

B: No, he didn't. He played the piano in 2004.

(3) _____ (he / play) the guitar in 2005.

A: (4) _____ (Grace / win) any awards?

B: Yes, she has. She plays tennis really well.

(5) _____ (she / win) a competition in 2003.

A: (6) _____ (Elena / visit) England?

B: Yes, (7) _____ .

A: How many times (8) _____ (she / be) there?

B: (9) _____ (she / be) there twice.

(10) _____ (she / go) there in 2003, and she went again in 2005.

A: (11) _____ (she / go) there in 2004?

B: No, she didn't.

Unit 7

Vocabulary

1 Do the crossword.

1 ___vaccination___

2 _____

3 driver's _____

4 _____ jacket

5 ____ – _____

6 _____ book

7 _____

8 insect _____

2 Look at the pictures of Joe's plans for a trip to Japan. Fill in the blanks with the nouns below.

blog   brochure   documentary   guide book   map   website

1 I've looked at a ___map___ to find the town I'm going to visit.

2 I've seen a good hotel in a _____ .

3 I've looked at a _____ about the country.

4 I've watched a _____ on TV about life in Japan.

5 I've bought a _____ on Japan.

6 I've designed a _____ . I'm going to write every day.

Extend your vocabulary

Grammar

1 **Match the statements with the question tags.**

1	You aren't hungry,	a	are they?
2	It isn't your birthday today,	b	isn't he?
3	Those students aren't English,	c	are you?
4	You're late,	d	isn't it?
5	It's cold in this room,	e	aren't you?
6	Your dad is a teacher,	f	is it?
7	These flip-flops are cheap,	g	is he?
8	He isn't friendly,	h	aren't they?

2 **Fill in the blanks with question tags.**

1 Ana runs fast, _____?

2 You live next to the police station, _____?

3 Maria doesn't have a driver's license, _____?

4 I speak English well, _____?

5 We need a new TV, _____?

6 You don't have a Japanese phrase book, _____?

3 **Complete these conversations with question tags.**

1 You don't feel well, _____*do you*_____?
   No, I don't!

2 He plays the guitar well, _____?
   Yes, he does!

3 Food is expensive in Japan, _____?
   Yes, it is!

4 She isn't a very good singer, _____?
   No, she isn't!

5 Those students come from China, _____?
   Yes, I think so.

6 These shoes are beautiful, _____?
   Yes, they are!

Vocabulary

1 Find six words in the word snake. Then fill in the blanks in the phrases below.

breakstrictobeybullyingresponsiblerespect

•••••••••• School rules ••••••••••

1 Always ____obey____ the rules.

2 There are _____ rules for uniforms, and you can't wear jewelry.

3 You have to be _____ for your homework. Don't cheat and copy from other students.

4 _____ other students isn't allowed. Be friendly and helpful.

5 Always _____ the opinions of the teachers and other students.

6 Never _____ the rules.

2 Match the phrases with the pictures.

drop litter on the floor   eat candy in the classroom   fight in the grounds   run in the corridor
shout in the cafeteria   wear makeup at school

1 ___shout in the cafeteria___

2 _____

3 _____

4 _____

5 _____

6 _____

Extend your vocabulary

Grammar

1 **Match these sentences.**

1 We don't have to eat at the school cafeteria.
2 Mom likes rock music.
3 I broke my sister's MP3 player.
4 We have to wear a uniform at my school.
5 My cousins go to a "free" school.
6 My brother and I have to be at home by nine o'clock.

a She lets me play my CDs as loud as I want.
b The school doesn't make them go to classes.
c The school doesn't let us wear street clothes.
d We aren't allowed to come back late.
e We're allowed to go out for lunch.
f Mom made me buy a new one.

2 **Complete Gemma's e-mail with the correct form of *be allowed to* in the affirmative or negative.**

	Me	My brother	My cousins
use chatrooms?	✓	✓	✗
go to bed late?	✗	✓	✓
have tattoos?	✗	✗	✓

Hi!
My name's Gemma. I'm 15. I (1) _'m allowed to_ use chatrooms, but I (2) _____ go to bed late. My brother (3) _____ go to bed late. It's not fair! My brother and I (4) _____ have tattoos. I don't mind. I hate tattoos! My cousins (5) _____ have tattoos, but they (6) _____ use chatrooms.

3 **Look at the pictures. Fill in the blanks with the correct form of *let* or *make* in the affirmative or negative.**

1 Mom _didn't let_ us watch the movie last night because it was late.

2 Dad _____ us clean our room and put away our clothes on Sundays.

3 Mom sometimes _____ me ride on her motorbike.

4 Our dog likes to come into my bedroom, but I _____ him sleep on my bed.

5 My parents _____ me play computer games on the weekends.

6 Yesterday, the teacher _____ me stay after school.

Unit 8

Vocabulary

1 Complete the verbs about Boris's future.

1 I'll _g r a d u a t e_ from high school.
2 I'll a_ _ _ _ _ for a job.
3 I'll b_ _ _ a house when I'm 30.
4 I'll g_ _ _ _ _ _ _ _ _ _ _ _ to my girlfriend.
5 I'll o_ _ _ _ a business. I want to sell computers.
6 I'll h_ _ _ _ two _ _ _ _ _ _ _ _ _ _. A boy and a girl.
7 I'll r_ _ _ _ _ _ from work when I'm sixty.

2 Label the pictures with the nouns below.

| accountant   architect   dentist   lawyer   mechanic   pilot   surgeon   TV reporter |

1 _mechanic_

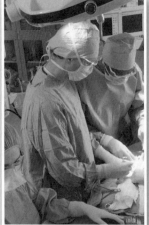

2 _____

3 _____

4 _____

5 _____

6 _____

7 _____

8 _____

Extend your vocabulary

Grammar

1 **Put the words in the correct order to make sentences.**

1 probably / Sara / pass the exam / won't
   Sara probably won't pass the exam .

2 to the party / will / Harry / come / probably
   _____ .

3 won't / definitely / be / late / we
   _____ .

4 I'll / study Japanese / I / next year / think
   _____ .

5 a new skateboard / buy / I'll / next weekend / definitely
   _____ .

6 I / go to the movies / think / don't / I'll / tonight
   _____ .

2 **Look at the chart. Write sentences about the future of these three students.**

	Jeff	Rosa	Ali
go to college?	✓✓	✓	✗✗
buy a house?	✗	✓	✓✓
work for a big company?	✓✓	✗✗	✗
open a business?	✗	✓✓	✓✓

✓✓ = definitely   ✓ = probably   ✗ = probably not   ✗✗ = definitely not

1 (Ali / go to college) *Ali definitely won't go to college* .
2 (Rosa / buy a house) _____ .
3 (Jeff / buy a house) _____ .
4 (Ali and Rosa / open a business) _____ .
5 (Rosa / work for a big company) _____ .

3 **Write sentences with the verb *think*.**

1 (Rosa / a house) *Rosa thinks she'll buy a house* .
2 (Ali / a big company) _____ .
3 (Jeff / a house) _____ .
4 (Rosa / college) _____ .
5 (Jeff / a business) _____ .

4 **You're talking to Rosa. Complete the questions.**

You: (1) *Will you* go to college? (go to college)

Rosa: Yes, I'll probably go to college.

You: (2) _____ ? (What / study)

Rosa: I'll probably study design.

You: (3) _____ ? (Why / study design)

Rosa: Because I love fashion! I want to design clothes.

You: (4) _____ ? (open a business)

Rosa: Yes, I'll definitely open my own business.

You: (5) _____ ? (be famous)

Rosa: No! I don't think I'll be famous. I just want to be successful.

Vocabulary

1 **Unscramble the words and fill in the blanks.**

1 The _population_ (nopupolita) of Mexico is about 107 million.

2 It's a good idea to _____(cerecly) old newspapers and bottles.

3 There's a lot of plastic and paper in household _____(bagreag).

4 Oil and coal are types of fossil _____(eluf).

5 Solar and wind power are types of alternative _____(gneery).

6 There's too much traffic in cities. It creates a lot of _____(nopullito).

7 There aren't many blue whales in the sea. Maybe they'll be _____(xencitt) in twenty years.

8 If global _____(minrwag) continues, there won't be much snow on the mountains.

2 **Look at the pictures. Fill in the blanks with the verbs below.**
What will happen in the future?

| burn decrease destroy freeze increase melt plant |

1 If the climate gets hotter, this ice will _melt_ .

2 If the climate gets colder, this lake will _____ .

3 More people will probably move to the cities. The population in cities will _____, but the population in the country will _____.

4 If people _____ a lot of wood, they'll _____ the forests. It's important to _____ more trees.

Grammar

1 **Circle the correct form of the verb in these sentences.**

1 If you (visit) / **will visit** this summer, we'll listen to some CDs together.

2 If the car starts, we **don't take / won't take** the bus.

3 If it **rains / will rain** this afternoon, we won't play tennis.

4 If my parents **come / will come** and pick me up, I won't call a taxi.

5 If I graduate next year, I **have / 'll have** a party.

6 If they **lose / will lose** the tickets, they won't see the match.

2 **Fill in the blanks with the correct form of the verbs below. Use the affirmative and negative.**

| be   give   go   miss   stop   study |

1 If it rains, we _won't go_ to the beach.

2 If the man drives too fast, the police _____ him.

3 If they _____ hard, they'll pass the exam.

4 If we run, we _____ late.

5 If my parents _____ me some money, I'll buy a new surfboard.

6 If she hurries, she _____ the bus.

3 **Complete these sentences.**

1 If I'm very tired tomorrow morning,
   I'll stay in bed . (stay in bed)

2 If I'm too busy on Saturday, _____
   _____ .
   (finish my homework on Sunday)

3 If Kate _____, we'll
   _____ .
   (not like the movie / go to a pizza restaurant)

4 If it _____, we'll
   _____ .
   (rain tomorrow / have lunch in the house)

5 If the swimming pool _____,
   _____ .
   (not open / we swim in the sea)

Unit 9

Vocabulary

1 Find eight nouns in the word snake. Then write them in the blanks in the sentences below.

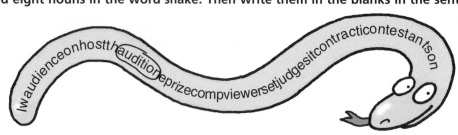

1 I went to an ___audition___ for a talent show.

2 We sang in front of three _____.

3 Twenty _____ were chosen to appear on the show.

4 The _____ introduced the show. She was very friendly and helped us relax.

5 There was a large _____ in the theater.

6 There were two million TV _____.

7 The _____ was $75,000.

8 The winner also got a recording _____.

Write the sentence hidden in the word snake. _____

2 Look at the pictures. Fill in the blanks with the verbs below.

> applaud   perform   rehearse   practice   print   vote

Extend your vocabulary

1 You have to ___practice___ for months for a talent show.

2 The day before, the competitors _____ in the studio.

3 You have to _____ in front of a big audience in the show.

4 If the people in the audience like you, they'll _____ for you.

5 TV viewers can _____ for their favorite singer.

6 Newspapers _____ photos of the winner the next day.

Grammar

1 Fill in the blanks with the correct form of the verb *be*. Use the affirmative and negative.

1 The TV company shows this program once a week. The program ___isn't___ shown every day.

2 This is an American newspaper. It _____ printed in New York.

3 A factory in China makes these CDs. They _____ made in England.

4 The winners _____ given a prize. They get $1,000 each.

5 You can only buy this book on the internet. It _____ sold in bookstores.

6 The judges don't decide who wins the competition. The winner _____ chosen by the TV viewers.

2 Write passive sentences about the school's prize day.

1 (They hold the event in the school auditorium.)
The event _is held in the school auditorium_.

2 (They clean the auditorium.)
The auditorium _____.

3 (They decorate the stage.)
The stage _____.

4 (They invite special guests.)
Special guests _____.

5 (They give prizes to the best students.)
Prizes _____.

6 (They print a photo of the event in the local newspaper.)
A photo of the event _____.

3 These sentences are wrong. Write the correct sentences.

> Gianni greets the customers.   Rita prepares the tables.
> Gabriella cooks the food.   Antonio serves the drinks.

1 The food is cooked by Gianni.
The food isn't ___cooked by Gianni___.
It's ___cooked by Gabriella___.

2 The tables are prepared by Antonio.
The tables aren't _____.
They're _____.

3 The drinks are served by Rita.
_____.
_____.

4 The customers are greeted by Gabriella.
_____.
_____.

Vocabulary

1 Circle (→ or ↓) six words in the wordsearch. Then write them in the sentences below.

I	N	S	P	I	R	E	D	U	T
M	T	R	O	U	B	L	E	T	H
P	Y	U	Q	V	U	P	G	I	O
R	E	B	C	R	L	E	A	C	K
O	E	X	P	E	L	L	E	D	I
V	U	W	S	K	I	P	P	E	D
E	N	A	C	Q	E	I	T	J	D
D	Y	M	O	T	D	Z	A	K	R

1 Tomiko was ___expelled___ from school because he broke the school rules.

2 Eva got into _____ at school because she was always late.

3 Tamsin didn't like school. She was _____ by a horrible student.

4 My English _____ a lot when I went to study in America.

5 David wants to play soccer for his country. He was _____ by Ronaldo.

6 Isabel _____ classes yesterday and went to the shopping mall.

2 Look at the pictures. Fill in the blanks with the verbs below.

> got a job   got his driver's license   failed   passed   quit his job   was promoted

1 Dan ___passed___ the exam.

2 Luisa _____ the exam.

3 Dan _____.

4 Dan is bored. He's going to _____.

5 Luisa _____ as a secretary.

6 Luisa _____. Now she's the manager!

Extend your vocabulary

Grammar

1 **Circle the correct form of the verb in these sentences.**

1 My brother's a good tennis player. He **inspired** / (**was inspired**) by Roger Federer.

2 The music prize **awarded** / **was awarded** to Caroline. She **played** / **was played** really well.

3 Charlie and Kathryn **didn't invite** / **weren't invited** to the party. They're angry!

4 Franz Ferdinand's first album **recorded** / **was recorded** in 2004. Over three million copies **sold** / **were sold**.

5 The concert **didn't hold** / **wasn't held** in the park. The musicians **performed** / **were performed** in the school hall.

2 **Look at the chart. Then fill in the blanks with the passive form of the verbs below.**

> design   discover   invent   paint   write

What?	Who?	When?
The Mona Lisa	Leonardo da Vinci, an Italian artist	1500–1504
The Cape Verde Islands	Diogo Gomes, a Portuguese explorer	1456
The Golden Gate Bridge	Joseph Strauss, an American designer	1937
The motorcycle	Gottlieb Daimler, a German engineer	1885
Romeo and Juliet	William Shakespeare, an English writer	1597

Portugiesisches Schiff des 15. Jahrhunderts.

1 The Mona Lisa ___was painted___ by Leonardo da Vinci.

2 The Cape Verde islands _____ by Diogo Gomes.

3 The Golden Gate Bridge _____ by Joseph Strauss.

4 The motorcycle _____ by Gottlieb Daimler.

5 Romeo and Juliet _____ by William Shakespeare.

3 **Look at the chart in exercise 2 again. Write negative and affirmative sentences.**

1 The Mona Lisa _wasn't painted_ 200 years ago. _It was painted 500 years ago_ .

2 The Cape Verde islands _____ by an English explorer. _____ _____ .

3 The Golden Gate Bridge _____ in 1947. _____ .

4 The motorcycle _____ in 1985. _____ .

5 Romeo and Juliet _____ by a Spanish writer. It _____ _____ .

Unit 10

Vocabulary

1 **Match the definitions with the phrases.**

1 become friends again
2 end a relationship
3 think someone is beautiful and interesting when you first meet
4 take a person as your husband or wife
5 legally end a marriage
6 speak angrily to someone when you disagree

a fall in love with
b have an argument with
c break up with
d get married to
e get divorced from
f make up with

2 **Look at the pictures. Fill in the blanks with the words below.**

cake   flowers   invitations   presents   reception   ring   wedding

Donna and Luis got married last week ...
1 They sent ___invitations___ to hundreds of people!
2 They chose a beautiful _____ .
3 The _____ was held in an old church.
There were _____ everywhere.
4 The _____ was held in a hotel.
Luis and Donna were given a lot of _____ .
There was a huge _____ !

Extend your vocabulary

Grammar

1 Circle the correct preposition.

1 Tina got divorced **to** / **from** her husband last year.

2 I don't want to talk to Rachel. I've had an argument **of** / **with** her!

3 Eric is unhappy. His girlfriend broke up **to** / **with** him yesterday.

4 What do you think **with** / **of** Salma's new boyfriend?

5 It was a great party, but the neighbors complained **about** / **from** the noise!

6 Do you want to go out with Lucy again? Why don't you make up **with** / **about** her?

2 Write sentences in the simple past with the words in parentheses. Use the correct prepositions.

1 Marie / have an argument / her boyfriend

   Marie had an argument
   with her boyfriend .

2 David / go out / Greta

   _____

   _____ .

3 Janet / fall in love / Brad

   _____

   _____ .

4 Nuno / introduce me / his friend

   _____

   _____ .

5 Serena / get married / Bill last Saturday

   _____

   _____

   _____ .

6 Gina and Vera / talk / Mark

   _____

   _____ .

3 Complete these conversations.

1 "What are they _talking about_ ?"
   "They're talking about the movie."

2 "Who's she _____?"
   "She's going out with Dave."

3 "Who's he having an _____?"
   "He's having an argument with his brother."

4 "Who does _____?"
   "She lives with her grandma."

5 "_____ did they _____?"
   "They complained about the noise."

6 "Who's _____?"
   "She's worried about Charlie."

Vocabulary

1 Unscramble the words and fill in the blanks.

1 Be quiet! Why do you ____keep____ (epek) shouting?

2 I've seen this movie before, but I don't _____ (dinm) seeing it again.

3 Cara has _____ (cdedied) to dye her hair red.

4 If you have a toothache, you should _____ (genarar) to see the dentist.

5 My parents can't _____ (dasnt) listening to rock music. They hate it!

6 Will you _____ (orimsep) to go to the concert with me.

7 I plan to visit Egypt next year. I'm _____ (destenteri) in seeing the Pyramids.

2 Look at the pictures. Fill in the blanks with the verbs below.

> an appointment   an argument   a chat   a date   a meeting   a talk

1 ____a meeting____

2 _____

3 _____

4 _____

5 _____

6 _____

Extend your vocabulary

Grammar

1 **Write sentences in the simple past with the verbs in parentheses. Use the *to* form.**

1 Tom and Janie _arranged to meet_ at eight thirty. (arrange / meet)

2 My parents _____ a new car last week. (decide / buy)

3 I _____ and see my grandmother. (promise / go)

4 Ben _____ the meeting at five o'clock. (plan / finish)

5 Patricia _____ to Erica on the phone, but she was too busy. (want / chat)

2 **Fill in the blanks with the *-ing* form of the verbs below.**

> learn   practice   swim   wait   watch

1 Do you enjoy ___watching___ talent shows on TV?

2 A lot of people want to buy tickets for this movie. Do you mind _____ in line?

3 If you want to be a good guitarist, you have to keep _____ .

4 I never go to the swimming pool. It's too cold. I can't stand _____ in cold water!

5 My brother is interested in _____ languages. He's studying Korean at the moment.

3 **Look at the pictures. Write sentences with the verbs in parentheses. Use the *to* or *-ing* form.**

1 I really _enjoy playing_ tennis. (enjoy / play)

2 I _____ part in competitions.
(like / take)

3 I always _____ . (hate / lose)
I always _____ ! (try / win)

4 I _____ in the U.S. (plan / live)
I _____ a professional tennis player.
(want / be)

Unit 11

Vocabulary

1 Circle (→ or ↓) eight types of sports equipment in the wordsearch. Then write the words.

1 c _a p_
2 s _ _ _ _ _ _
3 f _ _ _ _
4 s _ _ _ _ _
5 p _ _ _ _
6 g _ _ _ _ _ _
7 s _ _ _ _ _ _ _
8 m _ _ _ _

E	S		P	I	K	E	S		T
G	L	C	A	P	R	N	E		E
D	E	X	R	U	D	O	F
A	S	T	I	C	K	R	I
S	M	A	S	K	E	K	N
V	I	G	L	O	V	E	S
U	M	I	S	P	A	L	Y

Extend your vocabulary

2 Look at the pictures. Fill in the blanks with the adjectives below.

> complicated   exciting   lonely   muddy   powerful   rough   skillful

Soccer is an (1) _exciting_ sport.

Cricket is (2) _____ . There are a lot of rules!

Rugby is (3) _____ . The players get very (4) _____ !

Sailing is very (5) _____ when there isn't anyone on the yacht with you.

Motor racing is fast. The cars are very (6) _____ .

Golf is a very (7) _____ sport. You need to practice a lot to be a good player.

Grammar

1 Circle the correct words.

1 Has **anyone** / **everyone** seen my keys? I've lost them!
2 I'm not hungry. I don't want **anything** / **something** to eat.
3 I met **anyone** / **someone** from Panama last week.
4 I want to buy **anything** / **something** for my dad's birthday.
5 The kitchen is clean and I've put away **everything** / **anything**!
6 I can't find my glasses. I've looked **anywhere** / **everywhere** for them.

2 Fill in the blanks with the correct form of the words in parentheses.

1 There ___is___ someone on the phone for you. (be)
2 Clara _____ something to wear for the party on Friday. (need)
3 Oliver's bedroom was a mess. Everything _____ on the floor! (be)
4 It's very dark. I can't_____ anything. (see)
5 Every year, Juan _____ somewhere interesting on vacation. (go)
6 _____ anyone _____ a pen? (have)

3 Fill in the blanks in these sentences with *someone, something, anyone* or *anything*.

1 I have to go, mom. There's _someone_ at the door.

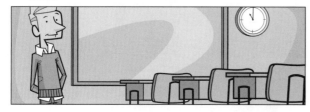

2 It's lunchtime. There isn't _____ in the classroom.

3 Is there _____ to drink?

4 Is there _____ at home?

5 There's _____ in that bag. What is it?

6 We're bored. There isn't _____ to do!

4 Complete the conversations using the verbs in parentheses and the pronouns below.

> anyone   everything   someone
> something   somewhere

Luis: I (1) _met someone_ (meet) cool last week. He's a rock star!
Sara: Where did you meet him?
Luis: I (2) _____ (go) downtown to see a band. I met him there.

Tony: I (3) _____ (see) fantastic in the sports store yesterday. It was a beautiful surfboard, but I didn't buy it. it cost $300.
Yuko: Did you (4) _____ (buy) from the store?
Tony: No. (5) _____ (be) too expensive!

Vocabulary

1 Fill in the blanks with the correct words below.

> court   field   goal posts   net   paddle   racket   referee   umpire

Rugby

1 You play on a ___*field*___. There
   are _____ at each end.
2 A _____ controls the
   match.

Table tennis

3 You hit the ball with a _____.

Tennis

4 You hit the ball with a _____.
5 You play on a _____. You
   have to hit the ball over the
   _____.
6 An _____ controls the
   game.

2 Look at the pictures showing sports equipment. Label the pictures with the words below.

> bat   flag   glove   helmet   pads   whistle

Extend your vocabulary

Match officials

2 _____

1 ___*flag*___

Football

3 _____

4 _____

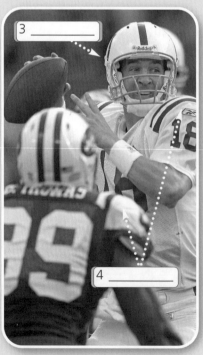

Baseball

5 _____

6 _____

Grammar

1 Circle the correct words.

1 Smallville is the town **which** / **where** my uncle lives.
2 Baseball is the sport **who** / **which** I like best.
3 Mrs. Jones is the lady **who** / **which** teaches us English.
4 This is the bus **where** / **which** stops outside my house.
5 The car won't start. We need someone **who** / **which** can fix cars!
6 Sportsworld is the store **which** / **where** I bought my new skateboard.

2 Fill in the blanks with *who, where* or *which.*

1 An architect is a person ____*who*____ designs buildings.
2 That's the hospital _____ my dad works.
3 Ice hockey is a sport _____ originated in Canada.
4 This is the park _____ we play soccer on the weekend.
5 I don't know anyone _____ can speak Chinese.
6 Look! These are the shoes _____ I bought yesterday.

3 Look at the picture. Write sentences using relative pronouns.

1 This is a room. The customers eat here.
This is the room *where the customers eat* .
2 Eddie is a young man. He serves the customers.
Eddie is the young man _____ .
3 This is wood. It goes in the stove.
This is the _____ .

4 Joanna is a woman. She prepares the pizzas.
Joanna is the _____ .
5 This is a machine. It makes coffee.
_____ .
6 This is a refrigerator. They keep the food here.
_____ .

Unit 12

Vocabulary

1 Do the crossword.

1 → There are classrooms, a gym and tennis courts on our school __*campus*__ .

1 ↓ The _____ center is a place where people can meet.

2 People who live on the streets can sleep at the homeless _____ .

3 Very poor families often live in a _____ .

4 A _____ home is a good place for old people who need a lot of help.

5 If you want to visit someone who lives in a _____ community, you have to ask the guards to let you in.

Extend your vocabulary

2 Look at the pictures. Label the picture with the words below.

balcony   driveway   fence   garage   gate   porch   steps

1 __*balcony*__

2 _____

3 _____

4 _____

5 _____

6 _____

7 _____

Grammar

1 How would you improve your neighborhood? Match the sentences.

The problems …

1 It's dirty.
2 There's too much traffic.
3 People don't have anywhere to meet.
4 There's litter everywhere.
5 Young people don't have anything to do.
6 There's a lot of crime.

The improvements …

a I'd build a community center.
b I'd put more police on the streets.
c I'd organize a soccer team.
d I'd clean the streets.
e I wouldn't allow too many cars.
f I wouldn't let people throw things on the ground.

2 Put the words in order. Then fill in the blanks in the conversation.

A: You're the new principal! (1) What ___would you change___ (you / change / would / what) at your school?

B: (2) _____ (build / I'd / a bigger gymnasium). The one we have is too small!

A: (3) _____ (the lessons / would / be) different?

B: I think languages are important. (4) _____ (learn / students / would) two or three
languages, and (5) _____ (visits / I'd / arrange) to other countries, too.

A: (6) _____ (you / would / change) the school rules?

B: (7) _____ (change / I / wouldn't) many rules. But (8) _____
(would / finish / classes) earlier!

3 Fill in the blanks in the conversations with *would* and the correct form of the verbs in parentheses.

Ana: (1) _Where would you go_ (where /
go) for your ideal vacation?

Rob: (2)_____ (travel) to
Jamaica. I love reggae!

Ana: What about Europe?
(3) _____ (visit)
England?

Rob: I don't know. (4)_____
(not go) anywhere cold. I don't like
cold weather!

Rob: (5)_____ (what / do) with a
thousand dollars?

Ana: (6)_____ (buy) a new laptop. I love
computers!

Rob: What about clothes?

Ana: (7)_____ (not buy) any more
clothes. I already have a lot of clothes!

Vocabulary

1 Find six words in the word snake. Then fill in the blanks in the sentences.

exercise friends living part volunteer exams

1 Paulo is doing ___volunteer___ work in Africa for a month.
2 Abdul often takes _____ in events for charity. He wants to help people.
3 Cassie makes a lot of _____ at the community center.
4 When I finish university, I want to make a _____ as a musician.
5 At the end of every school year, we take _____ to check that we're making progress.
6 Lisa isn't fit. She's going to do some _____ in the gym.

2 Look at the pictures. Fill in the blanks with the expressions below.

make up   put on   take off   turn off   turn on   work out

1 Come on! _Make up_ your mind!

2 I can't see anything. _____ the light!

3 Don't use a calculator. _____ the answer yourself!

4 It's late. _____ the TV and go to bed!

5 It's cold. _____ your gloves!

6 Would you like to _____ your coat?

Grammar

1 Circle the correct form of the verbs.

1 Dana's lazy. If she studied harder, she **'ll get** / **'d get** better grades.

2 If we **have** / **had** a swimming pool in our garden, I'd go swimming every day.

3 If you put on your coat, you **wouldn't feel** / **don't feel** so cold.

4 You're a good singer. If you **'d go** / **went** to the audition, the judges would choose you for the show.

5 My neighbors are noisy. If they **were** / **are** quieter, I'd sleep better.

6 If I lived nearer my girlfriend, I**'d see** / **'ll see** her every day.

2 Fill in the blanks with the correct form of the verb in parentheses.

1 I don't have any money. I can't buy a ticket for the concert. (have / buy)

If I had some money, I'd buy a ticket .

2 Ben plays the guitar badly. He doesn't practice every day.

If he _____ every day, he _____ better. (practice / play)

3 Mariella always gets up late, and she arrives at school late.

If she _____ earlier, she _____ late. (get up / not arrive)

4 I want to take a photo, but I don't have my camera with me.

If I _____ my camera with me, I _____ a photo. (have / take)

5 He wants to buy a sports car, but he isn't rich.

If he _____ rich, he _____ a sports car. (be / buy)

6 Jeff often breaks the rules. He gets into trouble.

If he _____ the rules, he _____ into trouble. (not break / not get)

3 Look at the picture. What are the people thinking? Complete the sentences.

1
It isn't sunny! I can't go to the beach.
If it was sunny, I'd go to the beach .

2
We don't live near a town! We can't go shopping. If _____, we'd go shopping.

3
I don't have any CDs! I can't listen to music. If _____ _____, _____ to music.

4
There isn't a computer! I can't e-mail my friends. If there _____ _____, I'd e-mail my friends.

6
We don't have any food in the apartment!
I can't cook a meal. If _____ some food, _____.

5
The water is cold! I can't swim in the pool. If _____ _____ warm, _____.

Extra reading 1

Dead Man's Island

We went to Scotland the next day, first by plane, then by train. Greta Ross travelled with us.

I looked out of the train window and saw fields and villages and mountains. "Mum is right," I thought. "Scotland is a very beautiful place."

"You're going to be my husband's secretary," Greta Ross told my mother. "He's a businessman, but he never leaves the island. He does all his work by telephone and letter and computer. He invests money in companies, all over the world."

"Do many people live on the island?" I asked.

"Not many," said Greta Ross. "You'll meet them soon."

"Greta Ross is young," I thought. "Is her husband young, too? How can a young man buy an island? Is he very rich?"

After the train, we went on Mr. Ross's boat, which took us out to the island. The boatman was a young man. He had dark hair and was brown from the sun.

"This is Tony," said Greta Ross. "He works for Mr. Ross."

"Hi," said Tony.

Soon we were near the island. I could see the beaches and the cliffs. The boat slowed down.

"There are dangerous rocks around the island," explained Tony. "A lot of them are under the water and you can't see them. I have to be careful. But the rocks keep other boats away, and that pleases Mr. Ross."

"Why?" I asked.

Tony looked at Greta Ross, but she wasn't listening.

"Mr. Ross doesn't like visitors to the island," Tony said in a quiet voice.

Then Greta Ross looked at us and Tony said no more.

"Why doesn't Mr. Ross like visitors?" I thought. "Has he something to hide?"

When we arrived on the island, my mother and I followed Greta up to the house. It was very big and there were trees all around it.

A woman was waiting inside the house.

"This is Mrs. Duncan, Tony's mother," said Greta. "She's the housekeeper and her husband is the gardener. Mrs. Duncan will take you up to your rooms. I'm going to tell Mr. Ross you've arrived."

The housekeeper was a little woman with short hair. She went up the stairs, and my mother and I went after her.

My room was next to my mother's. I looked out of the window and saw the gardens at the back of the house. A man was working in the garden, near some trees. "Is that Mr. Duncan?" I thought. I looked between the trees and saw the sea. "It's a beautiful house and a beautiful island."

1 Circle T (True) or F (False).

1 Mr. Ross travels a lot. T / **F**

2 The sea around the island is dangerous. T / F

3 A lot of people live on the island. T / F

4 Mr. Ross lives in a big house with a garden. T / F

2 Fill in the blanks with the verbs in the box.

> be   keep   like   travel   work

The girl and her mother (1) _traveled_ to the island by boat. The girl's mother is going to (2) _____ for Mr. Ross. The boatman has to (3) _____ careful, because there are a lot of rocks in the water. Other boats (4) _____ away from the island. Mr. Ross prefers that, because he doesn't (5) _____ visitors.

3 Soon they will meet Mr. Ross. What sort of person do you think he is? Write Y (yes) or N (no) for each adjective.

friendly ☐   sad ☐   strange ☐

busy ☐   old ☐   angry ☐

Extra reading 2

The Children of the New Forest

One day in November 1647, Jacob Armitage hurried through the New Forest to the house of Arnwood.

"You must leave this house immediately," he said to Edward Beverley. "Come with me to pack your things. You must come to my home and stay there."

"But why, Jacob?" Edward asked the old man. "Why?"

"The King has escaped from his prison at Hampton Court," Jacob explained. "He's riding south through the forest, and Cromwell's soldiers are searching for him. And I've just heard a group of soldiers in the forest – they were talking about Arnwood. They know that your father was the King's friend, and they're planning to burn Arnwood tonight, because they think the King is hiding here."

"Burn Arnwood! They can't do that! It's my house, and I'm staying here!" Edward said angrily. He was fourteen years old, the oldest of the four Beverley children.

The Beverley children lived alone at Arnwood, with an old woman who did the cooking and all the work of the house. Their father, Colonel Beverley, was killed while fighting for King Charles I at Naseby in 1645. Before he left home, he asked Jacob, a poor forester who lived near Arnwood, to look after his family. Jacob knew the family well and was happy to do this. And when the children's mother died a few months later, Jacob came every day to visit the children and to help them.

"My dear boy," Jacob said, "remember your sisters and brother. The soldiers will shoot them, or burn them in the house. No, no, you must all come with me."

In the end, Edward agreed. He and his brother Humphrey, who was twelve, packed their things. Then they put them on Jacob's horse, White Billy, who was waiting outside.

Jacob told Alice, who was eleven, and Edith, who was eight, that they were going to visit his home in the forest. He did not tell them about the soldiers.

"Edward, here is my key," said Jacob quietly. "Lock the door of the house, and take my gun from the wall. Don't leave your brother and sisters. I'll help the cook to pack her things, and then I'll follow you."

The four children left the big house and went into the forest with White Billy. It was five o'clock in the afternoon, and already dark. Jacob helped the cook, who hurried away to her family in Lymington, and then he hid in the trees near the house, and waited.

After a while he heard horses, and the Parliamentary soldiers arrived. Soon they were in the gardens and all round the house. A few minutes later Jacob saw black smoke going up into the sky; then he saw flames at the windows. Arnwood was burning!

1 Match the people with the sentences.

1 Cromwell's soldiers   a ... has a horse called White Billy.

2 Jacob Armitage   b ... has escaped from prison.

3 Edward's parents   c ... don't like the King or his friends.

4 The King   d ... live at Arnwood.

5 The Beverley children   e ... are dead.

2 Circle T (True) or F (False).

1 At first, Edward wants to stay at Arnwood. **T** / F
2 The children go to stay at Jacob's house. T / F
3 The King's soldiers burn Arnwood. T / F
4 Jacob dies in the fire at Arnwood. T / F

3 What do you think will happen in the story? Check (✔) Yes, Maybe or No for each sentence.

	Yes	Maybe	No
1 The soldiers will find Jacob and kill him.	☐	☐	☐
2 The King will go back to prison.	☐	☐	☐
3 Edward will become a soldier.	☐	☐	☐

Extra reading 3

The Wind in the Willows

The Mole worked very hard all morning, cleaning his little home. He brushed, and he washed; he cleaned the floors and the walls, he stood on chairs to wash the tops of cupboards, he got under the beds, he took up the carpets. He cleaned and he cleaned, until his arms and his back ached with tiredness.

It was springtime, and the smell and the sound of spring were everywhere, even in the Mole's dark little house under the ground. And with the spring comes the promise of change, of sunshine, of new green leaves. So it was not surprising that the Mole suddenly put down his brushes and said, "Oh bother!" and then, "I'm tired of cleaning!" Something up above the ground was calling to him, and he ran out of his house and began to dig his way upwards to the sun.

He dug and he pushed, and he pushed and he dug. "Up we go! Up we go!" he said to himself, until at last his nose came out into the sunlight, and he found himself in the warm grass of a field.

"This is fine!" said the Mole. "This is better than cleaning!" The sunshine was warm on his back and the air was filled with the songs of birds. He gave a little jump for happiness, shook himself, and then began to cross the field towards some trees. Here and there he went, through the fields and the woods, looking and smelling and listening. Everywhere animals and birds were busy, talking and laughing, looking for food, making new homes for the spring. The Mole enjoyed it all.

Then, suddenly, he came to a river. He had never seen a river before in his life – this wonderful bright shining thing, which danced its way in and out of the shadows under the trees. It was never still for a minute, hurrying and laughing and talking to itself.

And at once, the Mole was in love with it. He walked along the river bank, listening and watching all the time. At last he sat down on the grass and looked across the river to the bank opposite. There was a dark hole in the bank, and the Mole watched it dreamily, thinking that it would be very pleasant to have a little house by the river. As he watched, he saw something shining in the hole. Soon he saw that it was an eye, and then a face appeared as well.

A brown little face, with whiskers.

With bright eyes, and small ears, and thick shiny hair.

It was the Water Rat!

Then the two animals stood up and looked at each other.

"Hello, Mole!" said the Water Rat.

"Hello, Rat!" said the Mole.

"Would you like to come over?" asked the Rat.

"Oh, it's easy to talk," said the Mole, a little crossly. The river was new to him and he did not know how to get to the other side.

The Rat said nothing, and disappeared. Then he appeared again, in a little blue and white boat, which came quickly across the river towards the Mole. It stopped by the bank, and a moment later the Mole, to his great surprise and excitement, found himself actually sitting in a real boat.

1 Circle the correct answer.

1 The Mole lives …
   a in the river.   b underground.   c in a tree.

2 The Water Rat lives in a hole in …
   a a wall.   b a tree.   c the river bank.

2 Put the sentences in the correct order.

A The Mole sees the Water Rat. ____

B The Mole comes to a river. ____

C The Mole sits in the boat. ____

D The Mole cleans his home. _1_

E The Water Rat crosses the river in a boat. ____

F The Mole pushes through the ground and comes out in a field. ____

3 What do you think the Mole and the Water Rat will do next? Check (✔) *Yes* or *No* for each sentence.

	Yes	No
1 They'll have a picnic.	☐	☐
2 They'll fall in the river.	☐	☐
3 They'll meet some other animals.	☐	☐

Extra reading 4

Skyjack!

1

The air hostess smiled. "Welcome aboard, sir. Would you like a newspaper?"

"Yes, please." Carl took the newspaper and looked at his ticket. "I'm in seat 5F. Where's that?"

"It's near the front of the plane, sir. On the left, there. By the window."

"I see. Thank you very much." Carl smiled back at the air hostess. She was young and pretty. Just like my daughter, he thought.

He put his bag under his seat and sat down. His friend Harald sat beside him. They watched the other passengers coming onto the plane. Harald looked at his watch.

"9.30 p.m.," he said. "Good. We're on time."

Carl agreed. "And in three hours we'll be home," he said. "That's good. We've been away for a long time. You'll be pleased to see your family, won't you, Harald?"

Harald smiled. "Yes, I will. Have you seen this, sir?" He opened his bag and took out two small planes. "These are for my sons. I always bring something back for them."

"How old are your sons?" Carl asked.

"Five and almost seven. The older one has a birthday tomorrow."

"He'll be very excited tonight then."

"Yes. I hope he gets some sleep."

The plane took off. Carl watched the lights of the airport grow smaller below them. Then the plane flew above the clouds and he could see the moon and the stars in the night sky. He lay back in his seat and closed his eyes.

2

Later, he woke up. Harald was asleep. Carl looked at his watch. It was midnight. He called the air hostess.

"Excuse me. What time do we arrive?"

"11.30 p.m. local time, sir. That's about half an hour from now."

"Thank you.' Carl changed the time on his watch.

"Anything else, sir?"

"No, I don't think so. Oh, wait a minute – could I have a cup of coffee, please?"

"Yes, of course, sir.' He watched her bring the coffee. "She walks like my daughter, too," he thought. "And she is very young. She looks nervous, not sure what to do."

"How long have you been an air hostess?" he asked.

She smiled. "Three months, sir," she said.

"Do you like it?"

"Yes, I love it. It's very exciting." She smiled nervously. "Will that be all, sir?"

"Yes, thank you."

"Have a nice flight."

He drank the coffee and started to read his newspaper. When Harald woke up, Carl showed him a page in the paper.

"Look. There you are," he said. He pointed to a picture. In the middle of the picture stood Carl himself – a short thin man with grey hair, wearing a suit. Behind him, on the left, was Harald – a tall, strong young man, like a sportsman. Both men were smiling. "That's you and me, outside the Embassy," said Carl. "We're in the news again. You can show it to your sons. You're a famous man, Harald!"

Harald laughed. "You're the famous man, sir, not me," he said. "I'm just a police officer. It's my job to take care of you. That's a photo of you, not me."

"Perhaps. But your children think that you're a famous man, I'm sure. Here, take it, and show it to them."

"OK. Thanks.' Harald smiled, and put the newspaper in his coat pocket. "I think I'll have a cup of coffee too." He called for the air hostess, but she did not come. Harald looked surprised.

"What's the matter?" Carl asked.

"The air hostess,' Harald said. "She's sitting down talking to those two men."

Carl looked up and saw the young air hostess. She was sitting in a seat at the front of the plane with two young men. They looked worried and nervous. Suddenly, one of the young men picked up a bag and walked into the pilot's cabin! The other man and the air hostess followed him.

"That's strange," said Carl. "What are they doing?"

"I don't know. It's very strange," said Harald. "I don't like it at all." He began to get out of his seat, but then stopped and sat down again.

For one or two minutes nothing happened. None of the other passengers moved or spoke. They had seen the young men too. It became very quiet in the plane.

A bell rang, and for a moment they could hear two voices arguing. Then the pilot spoke.

"Ladies and gentlemen, this is the Captain speaking. Please do not be afraid. There is a change of plan. We have to land at another airport before we finish our journey. There's no danger. We will land in fifteen minutes. Please stay in your seats and keep calm. Thank you."

Then the air hostess came out of the cabin. She looked very different now because she had a machine gun in her hand. She stood at the front of the plane and watched the passengers carefully.

1 **Circle T (True) or F (False).**

1 Carl and Harald are flying home. T / F
2 The flight normally takes half an hour. T / F
3 Harald is a police officer. T / F
4 Harald has two daughters. T / F
5 Carl is a famous man. T / F

2 **Fill in the blanks with the words and phrases below.**

> airport   bag   bell   cabin   cup of coffee
> machine gun   plan   young men

Harald wants a (1) _cup of coffee_ . He calls the air

hostess, but she doesn't answer. She's with two

(2) _____ . They walk into the pilot's

(3) _____ . One of them is carrying a

(4) _____ . Soon, a (5) _____ rings

and the pilot tells everyone that there's a change of

(6) _____ . They're going to land at a different

(7) _____ . Then the air hostess comes out.

She's carrying a (8) _____ .

3 **What do you think will happen in the story? Check (✔) Yes, Maybe or No for each sentence.**

	Yes	Maybe	No
1 The air hostess will kill one of the passengers.	☐	☐	☐
2 The plane will crash.	☐	☐	☐
3 Harald will fight the air hostess and the two men.	☐	☐	☐